S0-BJN-614

Write It Right

Writing an Ad

DISCARDED

Public Library
Incorporated 1862
Barrie, Ontario

By Cecilia Minden and Kate Roth

CHERRY LAKE
Publishing

Published in the United States of America by
Cherry Lake Publishing
Ann Arbor, Michigan
www.cherrylakepublishing.com

Reading Adviser: Marla Conn MS, Ed., Literacy specialist, Read-Ability, Inc.
Book Designer: Felicia Macheske
Character Illustrator: Carol Herring

Photo Credits: © Samuel Borges Photography/Shutterstock.com, 5; © India Picture/Shutterstock.com, 7; © kikovic/
Shutterstock.com, 17

Graphics Throughout: © simple surface/Shutterstock.com; © Mix3r/Shutterstock.com; © Artefficient/Shutterstock.com; © lemony/
Shutterstock.com; © Svetolk/Shutterstock.com; © EV-DA/Shutterstock.com; © briddy/Shutterstock.com; © IreneArt/Shutterstock.com;
© VectorMine/Shutterstock.com

Copyright © 2019 by Cherry Lake Publishing
All rights reserved. No part of this book may be reproduced or utilized in any
form or by any means without written permission from the publisher.

Library of Congress Cataloging-in-Publication Data

Names: Minden, Cecilia, author. | Roth, Kate, author. | Herring, Carol, illustrator.
Title: Writing an ad / by Cecilia Minden and Kate Roth ; Illustrated by Carol
 Herring.
Description: Ann Arbor, Michigan : Cherry Lake Publishing, [2019] | Series:
 Write it right | Includes bibliographical references and index. |
 Audience: K to Grade 3.
Identifiers: LCCN 2018034540| ISBN 9781534142862 (hardcover) | ISBN
 9781534139428 (pbk.) | ISBN 9781534140622 (pdf) | ISBN 9781534141827
 (hosted ebook)
Subjects: LCSH: Advertising—Juvenile literature. | Advertising
 copy—Juvenile literature. | Creative writing—Juvenile literature.
Classification: LCC HF5829 .M37 2019 | DDC 659.1—dc23
LC record available at https://lccn.loc.gov/2018034540

Cherry Lake Publishing would like to acknowledge the work of The Partnership for 21st Century Skills.
Please visit *www.p21.org* for more information.

Printed in the United States of America
Corporate Graphics

Table of
CONTENTS

CHAPTER ONE

Be Persuasive

Have you ever talked your grandma into getting you a toy? Maybe you talked your best friend into joining a team. These are both examples of you being **persuasive**.

You see **advertisements** every day. We call them "ads" for short. Ads try to persuade you to do something.

Are you good at getting others to follow your ideas?

"Pop-up" ads are online advertisements.

CHAPTER TWO

The Way Ads Work

Look through magazines and newspapers. Which ads get your attention? Reading ads is a good way to learn how to write them. Sales ads try to persuade people to buy things. Other ads are not about sales. They are more like **announcements**. These ads tell people about upcoming events. These ads try to answer four questions:

1. *What* is happening?
2. *Why* should someone go to this event?
3. *Where* is this event happening?
4. *When* is this event happening?

What are ways newspaper ads get your attention?

Ads often list other information too. For example, a sales ad might include prices. An ad for a contest probably explains the contest's rules.

Most ads use persuasive words. Many include action words. "Come," "see," and "listen" are words that tell us to take action. Other phrases or groups of words have special meanings that also make them persuasive. A few examples are "new and improved," "this week only," and "experts agree."

See What Makes Ads Work!

HERE'S WHAT YOU'LL NEED:

- Three or four magazines
- Marker
- A pencil and paper (or a computer and a printer)

INSTRUCTIONS:

1. Look through the magazines and find five ads that grab your attention.
2. Think about why each ad gets your attention.
3. Use a marker to circle the information in each ad that answers the four questions.
4. List the persuasive words or phrases you notice in each ad.
5. Make a list of ideas for your own advertisement.

Ideas for My Advertisement

- School Play
- Track Meet
- Food Drive ✓
- School Elections

CHAPTER THREE

Your Attention Please!

Before you write an ad, you need to know your **audience**. What group of people are you trying to reach? Use words that will **appeal** to that audience. It is a good idea to keep your sentences short. This will help your audience read your ad more quickly.

Imagine your school is having a food drive. You want as many students as possible to donate canned goods for the local food bank. What could you say in an ad that would get the attention of other students? How could you persuade them to donate?

Write for Your Audience!

HERE'S WHAT YOU'LL NEED:

- A pencil and paper (or a computer and a printer)

INSTRUCTIONS:

1. List the purpose of your ad.
2. Name the audience you hope to reach with your ad.
3. List the questions your ad will answer for the audience.
4. List words and phrases that will get your audience's attention and persuade them to do something.
5. Write the first **draft** of your ad. Remember to keep your sentences short!

Sample Ad Outline

PURPOSE OF YOUR AD
To persuade students to donate canned goods for the food drives

YOUR AUDIENCE
Students at your school

QUESTIONS YOUR AD WILL ANSWER
- **What is happening?** "School food drive for local food bank"
- **Why should someone donate cans?** You will help people who cannot afford to buy their groceries.
- **Where is this event happening?** The Fairview School Gym
- **When is this event happening?** Saturday, December 6, from 8:00 a.m. to 4:00 p.m.

WORDS AND PHRASES THAT ARE PERSUASIVE AND GET ATTENTION
- "Support our community!"
- "Help the local food bank!"
- "Have a heart. Do your part."
- "What CAN you give?"
- "Give what you CAN!"
- "You CAN make a difference."

What CAN you give?

The Fairview Food Drive is Saturday, December 6!

The drive will be held in the Fairview School Gym
from 8:00 a.m. to 4:00 p.m.

You CAN make a difference
when you give what you CAN.

All donated cans will be brought
to the local food bank.

CHAPTER FOUR

Made You Look!

Now you have decided which words to use in your ad! You also need to choose a **design** that will make your ad persuasive. Your audience will see the design first. Then they will read the words.

Bold letters and bright colors get people's attention. Picking the right picture to appear on the ad is another important step. Choose the design carefully. Don't try to fit too many words and pictures into your ad. Try different styles until you figure out which one works best!

Make sure your words are clear and easy to read.

Sample Draft of Final Ad

What CAN you give?

The Fairview Food Drive is Saturday, December 6!

The drive will be held in the Fairview School Gym from 8:00 a.m. to 4:00 p.m

You **CAN** make a difference when you give what you **CAN**.

Soup

All donated cans will be brought to the local food bank.

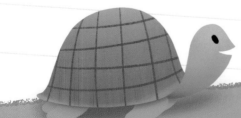

Decide on Your Design!

HERE'S WHAT YOU'LL NEED:

- Crayons or markers
- Paper (or a computer and a printer)

INSTRUCTIONS:

1. Try writing the words in different ways.
2. Try putting the words in different places on the paper.
3. Try different sizes and colors for the letters.
4. Try different pictures to go with your ad.
5. Make a **sketch** of the final ad.

CHAPTER FIVE

Bringing Everything Together

You are ready to do the final draft of your ad! Gather any materials you will need to do printing and create artwork. Have your first draft and your sketch handy. It is time to bring the words and the design together to share with your audience!

Make several rough drafts before choosing the final one.

Do the Final Draft!

HERE'S WHAT YOU'LL NEED:

- A copy of the first draft of your ad
- A copy of your design sketch
- Poster board or paper
- Crayons or markers
- Glue (if you are pasting pictures onto your ad)
- A computer and a printer (if everything has been done electronically)

INSTRUCTIONS:

1. Copy the words that will appear in your ad onto poster board or a new piece of paper.
2. Play around with the arrangement before making a final decision.
3. Glue or redraw your pictures on the poster board or paper.
4. Admire your ad!

What CAN you give?

The Fairview Food Drive is Saturday, December 6!

The drive will be held in the
Fairview School Gym
from 8:00 a.m. to 4:00 p.m

You **CAN** make a difference when you give what you **CAN**.

All donated cans will be brought
to the local food bank.

CHAPTER SIX

Final Check

ACTIVITY

Check Your Ad One More Time!

Ask yourself these questions as you reread your ad:

- Do I grab people's attention? (Ask a friend or family member if you are unsure!)

- Do I appeal to my audience?

- Do I give my audience all the information they need? (Think about whether you answer the four questions that ask what, why, where, and when.)

- Do I use persuasive words and phrases?

- Do I keep my sentences short?

- Do I use letters that are big and easy to read?

What should you do after you carefully check the final draft of your ad? Ask a teacher or parent if you should make copies. Discuss the best spots to place your ad. Pick areas where your audience is sure to see it. Does your school have a website? Ask your teacher if you can post your ad online.

What other ideas do you have for ads? Keep reading other people's ads and writing your own. Who knows? Someday you may get a job writing ads!

Sample Draft of Final Ad

What CAN you give?

The Fairview Food Drive is Saturday, December 6!

The drive will be held in the Fairview School Gym from 8:00 a.m. to 4:00 p.m

You CAN make a difference when you give what you CAN.

All donated cans will be brought to the local food bank.

One day your ads could become a commercial at the Super Bowl!

advertisements (ad-vur-TIZE-muhnts) public notices used to sell a product or make an announcement

announcements (uh-NOUNS-muhnts) written or spoken messages that tell people about events

appeal (uh-PEEL) to cause people to like someone or something

attention (uh-TEN-shuhn) the act of looking at or listening to something closely and carefully

audience (AW-dee-uhns) a group of people who view an ad

design (dih-ZINE) a plan for creating artwork and decorations

draft (DRAFT) an early version of a writing project

persuasive (pur-SWAY-siv) able to make people act or feel a certain way

sketch (SKECH) a rough drawing

BOOKS

Boucher, Francoize. *I Love Words*. Tulsa, OK: Kane Miller, A Division of EDC Publishing, 2010.

Connolly, Sean. *Advertisements*. Mankato, MN: Smart AppleMedia, 2010.

WEBSITES

Federal Trade Commission (FTC)—Admongo
www.admongo.gov
This site features sample ads and games that teach lessons about advertising.

PBS Kids Go!—Say? Cheese! How Ads Work
http://pbskids.org/fetch/ruff/find-what-you-want/ads-video.html
Watch this video that explains online advertising.

INDEX

About the AUTHORS

Cecilia Minden is the former director of the Language and Literacy Program at Harvard Graduate School of Education. She earned her doctorate from the University of Virginia. While at Harvard, Dr. Minden also taught several writing courses. Her research focused on early literacy skills and developing phonics curriculums. She is now a literacy consultant and the author of over 100 books for children. Dr. Minden lives with her family in McKinney, Texas. She enjoys helping students become interested in reading and writing.

Kate Roth has a doctorate from Harvard University in language and literacy and a master's degree from Columbia University Teachers College in curriculum and teaching. Her work focuses on writing instruction in the primary grades. She has taught kindergarten, first grade, and Reading Recovery. She has also instructed hundreds of teachers from around the world in early literacy practices. She lived with her husband and three children in China for many years, and now they live in Connecticut.